Trusting i

CW00662658

TRUSTING
IN GOD'S GRACE

SIMPLE
STEPS FOR
LETTING GOD'S
GRACE FLOW
THROUGH
YOU

DEREK PRINCE

TRUSTING IN GOD'S GRACE

Copyright © 1977 Derek Prince Ministries – International
This edition by Derek Prince Ministries

This edition DPM – UK 2018

Previously published under the title: The Grace of
Yielding

This book is an edited transcript from Derek Prince's message
The Grace Of Yielding recorded in 1974.

All rights reserved.

No part of this book may be reproduced or transmitted
in any form or by any means, electronic or mechanical,
including photocopying, recording, or by means of any
information storage and retrieval system, without permission
in writing from the publisher.

ISBN 978-1-78263-584-0
ePub: 978-1-78263-585-7
Kindle: 978-1-78263-586-4
Product code: B30

Derek Prince Ministries · www.derekprince.com

Set in Arno by Raphael Freeman, Renana Typesetting

Contents

Introduction

There are some things to which, as Christians, we should never yield. I do not believe that we should ever yield to Satan, for the Scripture says, "Resist the devil and he will flee from you." Nor do I believe that we should ever yield to sin, for the sixth chapter of Romans tells us that we are not to yield our members to sin. But there are circumstances and situations that occur in our lives which are only resolved when we learn to yield.

I find this is a mark of maturity which I look for in myself and which I esteem in others: knowing how to yield. I was listening once to a young preacher whom God has greatly blessed. He's a fine young man and God has done a great deal for him. But the whole theme of his preaching was what he could do. All of it was true and all of it was good. But I was sitting there saying to myself, "Brother, I'll be interested to see you come to the end of that." Because there's a place we eventually come to in the Lord where we've come to the end of what we can do. I'm not talking of what we can do merely by our carnal ability, or by education, but even in our ministry which is given us of God we come to a place, by divine appointment, where we can do no more. The trouble with many people is they've never recognised it.

What I'm sharing is the result of God's dealings with me over a number of years and I'm sure that God hasn't finished. I want to give you a number of Scriptures and then use a number of illustrations of "the grace of yielding" and its importance in the Christian life.

one

The Measure of Spiritual Strength

The first Scripture I want to examine in regard to our topic is Romans chapter 15, verse 1.

> *We then that are strong ought to bear the infirmities of the weak, and not to please ourselves.*

This, I believe, is the Scriptural mark of strength. It's not how much you can do, but rather how much you can bear the weakness of others. It's very satisfying to be strong in your own ability, in your own ministry, in your own experience and to be the person with all the answers. But that really doesn't require much spiritual strength. It does require spiritual strength to bear the weaknesses of others.

I believe that spiritual strength is measured by God and by the Scriptures in proportion to the amount that we are able to support and bear the weaknesses of other people. For me personally that has never been easy.

This is the exact opposite to the spirit of this age. The spirit of this age is, "Get what you can for yourself. Let the weak take care of themselves."

I've been meditating recently on the whole question of abortion, which to me is a most horrible, hateful evil. But if you discuss this issue with people, they'll justify it on the grounds that many unwanted children are not born into the world – maybe illegitimate children or children that are the result of problem homes or unsuitable mothers – they are never born. We just kill them off before they come out of the womb. I've learned by experience – regardless of what the Supreme Court or anybody else may say – that God classifies that as murder. This I've learned by experience, and I believe it's very clearly unfolded also in Scripture.

But the point I want to make just now is this: once we begin to make what suits us the measure of what is right, we're on a slippery path that goes downward to a horrible mess. Very, very quickly other issues will follow: "What about the child that is born hopelessly handicapped, that will never be more than a vegetable? Why should we keep that child alive?"

In the state of California there was a case before the courts of parents who deliberately did not feed a child that was born hopelessly incapacitated – they just allowed it to die. When we've dealt thus with the handicapped, we'll then proceed to deal the same way with the aged, the mentally sick, and so on. One after another they will be written off in the name of humanity.

I want to point out to you that this is not the Christian answer. It's not the Christian answer, not merely because abortion is forbidden by God, but also because the attitude behind it is totally unchristian. As Christians, we do not write the weak off. We don't even relegate them to an institution where we never hear about them or care about them again.

One of the outstanding marks of Christians in the first century was they cared for the weak. They cared for the sick. They didn't write them off. That's what really impressed the ancient world. They couldn't understand what made these Christians concerned about people who had nothing to offer – people who were only liabilities. But I've come to see that if we write off human liabilities, that's not strength – that's weakness.

It's the people who are liabilities, it's the incapacitated, it's the infirm, it's the weak believers who are the test of our spiritual strength. We have obviously come to a place in the United Kingdom, and in other countries too, where we cannot permit ourselves to live by the established standards of the age. If I'm a Christian, my first motive is not to get away with as much as I can legally get away with. My first motive is to please Jesus Christ in all that I do. Once we begin to live by seeking to please Jesus, we will inevitably lead a life that is completely different from that of the unconverted around us. We won't need to peddle a lot of doctrine, for in itself, pleasing Jesus will make us different.

two

Denying Ourselves

*P*aul says, "We ought not to please ourselves." Do you know what I've learned? I've learned that every time I do anything effective for God that's acceptable to Him, I begin by not pleasing myself. I've discovered this is an inevitable rule: every time I'm pleasing myself, I'm doing nothing that's worth anything to God. The first thing I've got to do is deny myself. This ego in me that is always asserting itself, saying, "I want, I wish, I feel, I think, If you ask me ... That's what I like ..." has got to be denied. I have to say, "No!"

There's no problem about what it means to deny yourself, for to deny is to say "no." All you have to do is say "no" to yourself. If you don't say "no" to yourself and keep saying "no" to yourself, you cannot lead a Christian life. You cannot be a self-pleaser and a Christ-pleaser. It's impossible.

These are the words of Jesus in Luke 9:23:

And he said to them all, if any man will come after me [this is absolutely universal], *let him deny himself, and take up his cross daily, and follow me.*

What is the first thing you do when you decide to follow Jesus? The first step. Let him do what? Deny himself. You cannot begin to follow Jesus until you make that decision. And then it goes on, "And take up his cross daily."

I never liked that word daily. For a long time I steered around that verse in Luke 9, because I knew another verse where it doesn't put the daily in. It's Matthew 16:24, where the same words are used, but without the daily. At that time my theology and my teaching was all built on a once-and-for-all experience of the cross, which is perfectly correct and theological. But it doesn't exhaust it. And here in Luke 9:23 Jesus sneaks in that little daily. "Let him take up his cross daily..." I believe every day presents every Christian with an opportunity to take up his cross. If you use the opportunity, you have a victorious day. If you lose the opportunity, you have a day of defeat.

But what is your cross? I heard a fellow preacher say it this way: "Your cross is where your will and the will of God cross." Your cross is the thing on which you can die. It's the place where you can lay down your life. When Jesus went to the cross He said, "No man taketh my life from me. I have power to lay it down, I have power to take it up." In this sense, no one will take your life from you. If you don't voluntarily lay it down, you'll still be in control of it.

Your cross, dear brother, is not your wife – unless you have power to lay her down and take her up day by day. Nor, dear lady, is it your husband. Nor is it the sickness you did not choose and cannot be healed of. Your cross is the place where you can make the decision not to please yourself.

In my own experience I could tell you how, time after time after time when I've had that inner struggle and made the right decision, blessing follows. Then – and not until then – I can minister. I cannot minister as long as I am pleasing myself. The old ego in me has nothing to give to anybody. He has to be dealt with before the ministry of God can flow out of my life. And Jesus reminds us, "You need to do it every day."

Many, many times you and I come to a situation in the day where God's will and our will cross. We have to see that as a God-given opportunity – not a disaster, but an opportunity.

three
_____

The Spirit of Christ

*T*his principle of taking up our cross and denying ourselves daily is the exact opposite of the way our natural mind works. It's diametrically opposed to the way the natural man thinks. I'd like to give you one or two other Scriptures which I find very challenging, very searching. The first Scripture I'll give, without going into the background or analyzing the content, is 1 Corinthians 1:25:

> *Because the foolishness of God is wiser than men; and the weakness of God is stronger than men.*

Now that's a paradox! There is a weakness that comes from God that is stronger than any strength we have. There is a foolishness that comes from God that is wiser than any wisdom we have. And there was one thing in which the weakness and the foolishness of God found their full expression. What was that? The cross! In the weakness and foolishness of the cross, God triumphed over all the strength and all the wisdom of this world. I believe God is asking you and me to learn that kind of weakness and that kind of foolishness.

It's never been an effort for me to be strong in my own personality. Furthermore God has blessed and used the strength I have. But God has shown me that it will only take me so far. If I wish, I can stop there. I am not compelled to go any further. I've seen many lives and ministries stopped at that point.

Now let's turn to another verse that touches on this – Romans 8:9:

> *But you are not in the flesh but in the Spirit, if indeed the Spirit of God dwells in you. Now if anyone does not have the Spirit of Christ, he is not His.*

This verse is strangely punctuated. It consists of two sentences separated by a full stop. If I had been responsible for the division into verses, I'd have made two separate verses out of these two sentences. As it stands, the first half of the verse speaks about "the Spirit of God"; the second half speaks about "the Spirit of Christ." I don't wish for a moment to suggest that there is any kind of division between these two; but I do believe there is a difference in the way that they represent the nature of God.

All through the Bible "the Spirit of God" is identified with "the Holy Spirit." It is the official title of the third Person of the Godhead – God the Spirit – the One who is co-equal with the Father and the Son and who speaks in the first person as God. For example, in Acts 13:2, the Holy Spirit spoke to the leaders of the church at Antioch and said, "Separate me Barnabas and Saul for the work whereunto I have called them." Here we have God Himself – God the Spirit – using the pronoun "I," speaking in the first person as God. The main emphasis is upon power and authority.

On the other hand, I believe "the Spirit of Christ" presents the divine nature specifically as it was manifested in the life of Jesus Christ. It cannot be separated from the nature and personality of Jesus. It is this kind of Spirit, Paul tells us, that marks the true child of God: "If any man have not the Spirit of Christ, he is none of his."

I believe – in fact, I know from direct observations – that there are many people who have been baptised in the Holy Spirit, who speak in tongues, who work miracles – but who demonstrate little or nothing of the Spirit of Christ. And the mark that makes us God's is not speaking in tongues, nor is it working miracles, nor is it preaching tremendous sermons. It's having the Spirit of Christ. If I were to ask myself what the Spirit of Christ was like, I would have to say it was a meek spirit, it was a humble spirit, it was a gentle spirit. It certainly was not arrogant, nor self-assertive, nor self-pleasing. And that, I believe, is what marks the true child of God: the Spirit of Christ.

We hear a good deal of teaching about claiming your inheritance, and getting what belongs to you. I've preached along that line many times myself, using such texts as the third epistle of John, verse 2: "Beloved, I wish above all things thou mayest prosper and be in health even as thy soul prospereth." Thank God, I believe it! But do you know, in God's sight you don't prosper by asserting your rights. The Spirit of Jesus did not lay claim to His rights. I believe prosperity, health, and inward peace and well-being of soul are the right of the new creation; but many times they are illegally appropriated by the old man for his own selfish purposes.

Today when I hear people say, "Brother, just claim it," something in me winces. When I hear those words, inwardly I picture an arrogant ego asserting its rights. How many of you would really like to live with somebody who's always "just claiming it"? Although all my claims may be fully legal, yet I am inwardly weary of the legalistic assertion of my inheritance in Christ.

I am weary, too, of continually having to instruct Christians on how to be healthy and how to prosper. Sure they need it, but brother and sister, when you learn how to be healthy and how to prosper, you are not out of primary school, spiritually. Your strength isn't what you have or what you can demonstrate. Your strength is the ability to bear the infirmities of the weak.

Now the Spirit of Christ was a spirit that freely yielded. Indeed, I believe He's the supreme example of yielding. It was just this aspect of His conduct that most clearly marked the difference between Him and Satan. It says in Philippians 2:6 about Jesus:

Who, being in the form of God, did not consider it robbery to be equal with God.

That is the New King James Version. But the New American Standard Bible says, "He did not regard equality with God a thing to be grasped." Do you see we have a complete specific contrast? Jesus was entitled to equality with God. It was His by divine nature, by divine right. He did not grasp at it. Lucifer, who became Satan, was not entitled to equality with God, but he did grasp at it, and he fell. The decisive point of difference was between grasping and yielding. I am exercised in my mind as to how much of our assertion and claiming and demanding is the expression of the Spirit of Christ and how much rather comes from the other source.

I'm convinced that the charismatic movement is going to have to face this issue. We are going to have to discern between true and false prophets, true and false ministries, those who are serving God in Spirit and truth, and those who are not. Miracles are not the decisive point of difference. The mark that separates is the Spirit of Christ: "If any man have not the Spirit of Christ, he is none of His."

Do you know what I believe about the charismatic movement? I believe it's just an interval between two waves. One wave has been going out, another wave is coming in. In between there's a mess, isn't there? A churning up, a lot of dirt and mire churned up, a kind of confusion, two forces going in opposite directions. That's the charismatic movement! It's not God's ultimate. Believe me, something else is coming which is going to be orderly, disciplined, Christ-honouring, and it's going to promote humility, brotherly love, and each esteeming others better than himself.

As far as I'm concerned the day of God's individual man of faith and power is on the way out. I say that without being critical of any man who may ever have qualified for that title. We need to realise that God works in different ways at different times. He doesn't go on forever doing the same thing. Some Christians are not prepared to accept that. They find a success formula, it works, and they go on until they've worked it to death.

I'm reminded of what Paul said to the men of Athens in Acts 17:30. Speaking about their many, many centuries of idolatry, he said, "The times of this ignorance God winked at." To wink is to close your eyes for a brief moment. So for a brief moment God voluntarily overlooked that ignorance.

Many people argue, "Well, God let me get away with it for ten years, so I'm going to go on getting away with it." No you aren't! God winked at it but now He's opened both His eyes; He's looking right at it and He says, "You'd better change." And when God says, "You'd better change," my advice is: change! If you don't, God has ways of pointing the lesson.

four

─────────

Being Willing to Yield

*N*ow I want to look at some examples of yielding, beginning with 1 Kings 3. In the first part of this chapter God appeared to Solomon in a dream and said, "Ask what you want." That would be a pretty difficult situation to find yourself in, when God suddenly says, "Now what do you want? I'll give it to you." You will remember Solomon did not ask for riches; he did not ask for honour; he did not ask for the lives of his enemies; but he asked for wisdom. He said, "Give me a wise and hearing heart." God was pleased with this choice and said: "Because you've asked for that I'll give you the other things you didn't ask for as well."

Shortly after, there came the case of the two women who were harlots, living together in one house. Each of them gave birth to a baby and each had the baby in bed with her. In the middle of the night one of the women rolled over on top of her own baby and killed it. In the morning there were two mothers with only one baby, and each of the mothers wanted the baby which was alive. The woman who was the real mother claimed the baby, but the mother whose baby had died said it was hers. So the case was brought before Solomon: these two women in court, and one baby. Solomon heard the case out. The real mother said, "It's my baby." The other woman said, "No, it's my baby." So Solomon said, "Well there's only one thing to do. Bring me a sword." When the sword came, he said, "I'll cut the baby in two, and each of you can have half." The woman to whom the baby did not belong said, "That's right, cut the baby in half and give me my half." But the real mother didn't want to see her baby die. She said, "No, give her the baby; let it live." Solomon said, "She's the mother!" As a result his wisdom became famous throughout Israel.

The lesson is very simple. If it's really your

baby, rather than see it die, you'll let the other woman have it. That's the real test. Many times in Christian service and ministry, a man brings forth something which is his, but somebody else contests it and claims it, and there's an argument and a fight. I could go through the history of the last thirty years and name man after man and case after case. That's when the real test comes. If it's your child, would you rather see the other woman have it than see it killed?

There are times when we are put to that test. Do I want to lay claim to my ministry and my success; do I want to establish my reputation? Or am I prepared to let somebody else have all that I worked for, all that I achieved, all that I prayed through? It depends on whether you love yourself more than the baby, or the baby more than yourself.

Next time you're faced with that situation, you'll be able to measure how real your love is. If you're willing to give it away, you love it. If you claim half, you don't.

I'd like to go for a moment to the story of Abraham in the 13th chapter of Genesis. Abraham had started out from Ur of the Chaldees in obedience to the Word of God, but not in full obedience. We see this from the 12th chapter of Genesis. There God said, "Get thee out from thy country, and from thy family, and from thy home, into a land that I will show thee." But Abraham did not fully obey God, because he took two extra persons with him – his father and his nephew. He was not authorised to take either. As long as he had his father with him, he only got halfway. He got to Haran, which is halfway between Ur and Canaan. He couldn't get any further until his father died.

Many of us are like that. God says, "Come out, leave everything behind; I'll show you your inheritance." But we want to take "Daddy" along. Daddy may be a promising career or a well-paid job or a denominational affiliation or a pension scheme. It may be one of many things. At any rate, God says, "As long as you take Daddy, you'll only get halfway." That's how it was with Abraham. He couldn't get into Canaan as long as he had his father with him. Stephen pointed this out in his speech to the Jewish council in Acts chapter 7. He said, "After his father died, he moved into the promised land."

But even so, Abraham still had a problem with him – his nephew Lot. Lot ought never to have been there. It wasn't long before both Abraham and Lot prospered. They both acquired so much cattle and so many goods that they could no longer live side by side as they had been doing. There was continual strife between their herdsman. We read what happened next in Genesis 13, beginning at verse 7:

And there was strife between the herdsmen of Abram's livestock and the herdsmen of Lot's livestock. The Canaanites and the Perizzites then dwelt in the land.

So Abram said to Lot, "Please let there be no strife between you and me, and between my herdsmen and your herdsmen; for we are brethren. Is not the whole land before you? Please separate from me. If you take the left, then I will go to the right; or, if you go to the right, then I will go to the left."

Abraham was the senior; he was the man whom God had called; he was the man to whom the inheritance belonged, but he stood back and said, "Lot, you make your choice. Whatever you choose, you can have."

> And Lot lifted his eyes and saw all the plain of Jordan, that it was well watered everywhere (before the Lord destroyed Sodom and Gomorrah) like the garden of the Lord, like the land of Egypt as you go toward Zoar. Then Lot chose for himself all the plain of Jordan, and Lot journeyed east. And they separated from each other. Abram dwelt in the land of Canaan, and Lot dwelt in the cities of the plain and pitched his tent even as far as Sodom. But the men of Sodom were exceedingly wicked and sinful against the Lord.

Now reading on after Lot was separated:

> And the Lord said to Abram, after Lot had separated from him: "Lift your eyes now and look from the place where you are – northward, southward, eastward, and westward; for all the land which you see I give to you and your descendants forever.

That was his inheritance. But until he had been willing to yield, God didn't show it to him.

That's how God will deal with us, too. As long as you hold on and say, "That's mine; I'm not letting go," you won't see what God has for you. It's the yielding spirit that receives the inheritance, not the grasping spirit, nor the grabbing spirit. As long as you continue to say, "It's mine and you can't have it; God gave it to me," you won't have what God has for you. You have to yield.

My wife, Lydia, often reminded me of an incident that happened in Palestine during World War II – before we were married. She was living at that time in a town named Ramallah, which is about ten miles north of Jerusalem. Though her main work was among children, a revival broke out among the Arab women in the city. It was a sovereign work of God, but my wife was the instrument that God used. Those Arab women would come in off the street unconverted, to be saved, delivered from evil spirits and baptised in the Holy Spirit – all in the one encounter. The work was flourishing and growing – a testimony to the Lord's grace.

But then a missionary who lived in Jerusalem claimed the work as his. He sent up an Arab worker and said, "This is our work. We had a worker in this town before you came." In actual fact, that particular worker had accomplished nothing of any lasting value, whereas my wife understood and loved those women and was loved by them. I bear testimony to this because twenty-five years later we went back to that village, my wife and I together, and when these women heard my wife was there they came running into the street to embrace her. They hadn't forgotten her twenty-five years later!

Be that as it may, my wife was confronted with this claim, and with the strength of a man against a single woman. So she said what Abraham said: "All right, you choose. And if you decide to go to the left, I'll go to the right." And the other missionary said, "Well, this is our work, we'll take it." So my wife said to the Arab women, "From now on we're having no meetings. The meetings are to be held at such and such a place; you go there and be faithful and support the work." After a year or two the work died completely because the worker who was sent to take it over had no real call from God. It was not his work. But my wife had won her own personal victory by yielding.

Meanwhile what happened was this. Within a few months, British and American soldiers serving in the countries of the Middle East began to find their way to that little home in Ramallah. They came there seeking God and the baptism of the Holy Spirit. In the next three or four years, scores and scores of American and British servicemen found God and were baptised in the Holy Spirit in that little children's home.

As a matter of fact, I myself was with the British forces in the Middle East at that time. I was stationed in the Sudan, right down almost in the centre of Africa. One day I met another Christian soldier who said, "If you want a real blessing, there's a little children's home ten miles north of Jerusalem – you should go there!" So as soon as my turn came, I took two weeks leave, and journeyed all the way down the Nile to Cairo and from there to Jerusalem. Finally I ended up in that little children's home and the blessing I got was greater than I had been expecting – it was my wife.

But the point of the story is this: by traditions and customs of the Middle East, those Arab women would never have been allowed in a place where British and American servicemen were coming. Had my wife held on to the women, the soldiers would never have come. But when we yield, then we get promoted. Many of those men, myself included, today are in full-time ministry all over the world: missionaries, pastors and so on; some in the United States, some in Britain, some in South Africa.

The lesson is: you have to be willing to let go. It's unfair, it's unreasonable, it's unjust! So what? God arranged it. He's in control. That's faith!

five

"Take Now Thy Son..."

*L*et us return to Abraham. Romans chapter 4 speaks about the steps of the faith of our father Abraham. One thing that has become very clear to me is that faith is not a static condition. It's not sitting on a church pew and saying, "I've got it." Faith is a walk in which one step follows another. Abraham is called the father of all of us who believe – if we walk in the steps of his faith.

Abraham's faith was progressive. If you go from Genesis chapter 12 to Genesis chapter 22, you see the various progressions of Abraham's faith. In chapter 22 his faith came to its grand climax. But what he did in chapter 22 he could never have done in chapter 12. His faith came to that climax because every time God said, "Step," he stepped. Every time God gave him a challenge, he accepted. So his faith was progressively built up. The Epistle of James says, "By works, his faith was developed and made mature." Faith is received as a gift but it's matured by walking in steps of obedience.

However, Abraham was human like the rest of us. He too made his mistakes. God had promised him a child of his own – an heir to take over his inheritance. But, as you know, the promise tarried. After twelve years, no heir had appeared. Sarah was 78 years old and she viewed the situation as hopeless. Finally she said, "If we're ever going to have a child, we'd better do something about it." When we deal with God, some of the most disastrous words that we can ever utter are, "We'd better do something about it."

Abraham took his wife's advice (which was a mistake) and had a child by Sarah's maid, Hagar. There was nothing immoral about that whatever. By the standards of the day it was right, moral and decent. But it wasn't the plan of God. The name of the child was Ishmael, and his descendants are numbered among the Arabs of the Middle East today.

Later, Sarah herself gave birth to Isaac – the child whom God had really intended her to have all along. For the succeeding four thousand years there has been tension between the descendants of these two children – Ishmael and Isaac – tension that seems to be coming to its climax in our day. By the irony of history the descendants of Ishmael now stand as the great barrier to the descendants of Isaac returning to their promised inheritance. History could not teach a plainer lesson: it is disastrous to grasp for a God-given inheritance by carnal means.

I heard another preacher say this: "The child of human expediency is an Ishmael." When you decide you'd better do something to help God, God help you! I was planning something once, and I went quite a long way in my plans. Then I got together with a fellow minister, and as we were talking it over, I said, "To tell you the truth, I don't think I'm going to do it."

He said, "Why not?"

"Well," I said, "I'm afraid it will be an Ishmael." I saw that my friend was impressed by that remark. Some time later we were together again and he said, "Would you mind telling me why you changed your mind about doing that thing?"

"It was the fear of the Lord," I told him. And I saw the answer satisfied him. I can sincerely say that I try to live in the fear of the Lord. I don't want to do anything that grieves God, that stands in God's way. I want to walk softly with the Lord. So I put my Ishmael in the pending file – which is where he is today!

To me, the basic lesson is this. The things that we think good, the things that seem right which are the result of human attempts to do the right thing are the biggest disasters. God keep us from them! God keep me from them! God keep you from them. God keep all of us from ever begetting an Ishmael because you will live to regret it.

What's the biggest test that God ever puts us through? In one word that begins with a "w": Waiting! When God tells you to climb the mountain, you start climbing immediately! But when God tells you to sit at the bottom and wait – you can't do it.

Probably the most mature character in the Bible is Moses. How did he mature? By forty years in the wilderness. What did it make him? The meekest man on earth. Moses didn't assert his rights; he stepped back and said, "let somebody else do it." I feel safe when I can say with all sincerity, "Let somebody else have the baby." Oh, I feel so safe! But when I'm nervous, tense and grasping, I'm headed for disaster.

Let's go back to Genesis chapter 22. God said to Abraham in verse 2:

> *"Take now your son, your only son Isaac, whom you love, and go to the land of Moriah, and offer him there as a burnt offering on one of the mountains of which I shall tell you."*

What was Abraham's response? The next verse tells us:

> *"So Abraham rose early in the morning and saddled his donkey..."*

One of the things you'll notice about Abraham was that he not merely obeyed God, but he obeyed God promptly. It's very conspicuous. When he was told to do something he got up early the next morning and did it. He didn't wait around until noon, wondering if God would change His mind. The next morning Abraham was up and on his way with Isaac for the three-day journey to Mount Moriah.

You know the story: they went up the mountain and Isaac said, "My father, here's the fire; here's the wood, but where's the lamb?" And Abraham said, "My son, God will provide a lamb." In the eleventh chapter of Hebrews the writer tells us that it was by faith Abraham was willing to offer his son to God and kill him, "accounting that God was able to raise him up, even from the dead." If you read the 22nd chapter of Genesis carefully, you will understand why the writer of Hebrews said that. It was because Abraham said to the men whom he left at the foot of the mountain, "We will go up, we will worship, and we will come down." Bless God! He really believed that even if he thrust that knife into his son, both of them would come down again. He had come to the place where he was actually ready to kill the miracle child who was the only hope of his God-promised inheritance, trusting God to bring him back to life again.

As he had the knife raised, ready to plunge it into his son, the angel of God called to him from heaven and stopped him. Abraham discovered that God had indeed provided an alternative sacrifice – a ram caught by its horns in a thicket. He offered that up to God in place of his son. After that, God spoke to him the second time:

> *Then the Angel of the Lord called to Abraham a second time out of heaven, and said: "By Myself I have sworn, says the Lord* [the writer of Hebrews says he swore by Himself because he could not swear by anything greater], *because you have done this thing, and have not withheld your son, your only son – blessing I will bless you, and multiplying I will multiply your descendants as the stars of the heaven and as the sand which is on the seashore; and your descendants shall possess the gate of their enemies.*
>
> Genesis 22:15–17

That's a strange thing, isn't it? Isaac was God's gift to Abraham and Sarah. They could never have had him apart from the miraculous intervention of God. He was supernaturally born. Yet the very child that God had given them God asked them to give back to Him as a burnt sacrifice.

I've tried to put myself in Abraham's position on his way to Mount Moriah and imagine what he was reasoning and thinking on the three-day journey.

"Why would God want Isaac? Didn't God give Isaac to us? Isn't he the promised one? Isn't he the only way that we'll ever receive our God-given inheritance? Haven't we left everything? Haven't we followed Him? Haven't we obeyed Him? Why should He demand Isaac?"

I don't know whether he thought or said that. But when he came to the place where he was willing to do what God had commanded, God spoke and said, "That's all right; now I know your heart. From now on, Abraham, I'll bless you as you've never been blessed before. And I will multiply your seed." What was his seed? Isaac. Do you understand the lesson? If he had held onto Isaac, all he'd have had was Isaac. When he gave Isaac up, he got Isaac back multiplied beyond his power to calculate.

I've seen that this is what happens when God gives us something very special for ourselves. It's from God. It's precious. It's unique. It's miraculous. But one day God is going to say,

"I want it. Give it back. Kill it. Lay it on the altar."
At that point you're either going to follow the
footsteps of Abraham, or you're going to miss
God's blessing.

I have to say that I've seen many servants of
the Lord make the bitter mistake of holding onto
Isaac – and all they are left with is Isaac. That is
the biggest test that comes to any servant of God:
Is he willing to put his ministry on the altar?

I can look back and see how I faced this test
in my own experience. Many of you know how I
became deeply involved in the ministry of deliverance and was publicly identified with it across
the United States. I can echo the words of Paul
and say that I've fought with wild beasts for the
truth of deliverance. I have fought physically,
I've fought spiritually, I've fought in prayer, I've
fought in fasting.

But there came a time when God joined me
with three other men who had nationally-known
teaching ministries. God sovereignly brought us
together in a relationship of mutual commitment
and submission. This was a sovereign dealing
of God with each and all of us – not anything
that we had planned or expected or even really

understood. In that sense, I would have to say, it bore the marks of an Isaac, not an Ishmael.

It wasn't long before I realised that my ministry of deliverance was included in the commitment I had made to my brothers. It had to be submitted to them. After much heart searching, I finally said to them, "Brothers, if you find that my ministry of deliverance is unscriptural or wrong and you take exception to it, I will not practice it." Do you think that didn't cost something? It did!

But today I praise God for the results which flowed from it. First of all, my brothers never asked me to give up practising deliverance. On the contrary, they supported me and strengthened me. When I was publicly attacked, they stood by me – often at the cost of their own reputation.

But beyond all that, something happened to the ministry of deliverance across the United States that I could never have achieved by my own efforts. When I gave God my Isaac, He multiplied it. Today the ministry of deliverance has been established in almost every area of the United States. I can go almost anywhere and preach deliverance, and there are qualified, dedicated men of God who will do the work. In fact, I very seldom have to minister deliverance myself any longer. God has raised up an army of men, willing and able to practice it. But believe me, it wasn't that way thirty years ago! Looking back now, I thank God I was willing to give Him my Isaac and let Him multiply it. I believe that if I'd held onto my Isaac, I would be left today with just my own ministry, isolated from the Body of Christ and from the mainstream of God's purposes.

Let's look in John 12:24 at the words of Jesus.

Most assuredly, I say to you, unless a grain of wheat falls into the ground and dies, it remains alone; but if it dies, it produces much grain.

I have always applied that to the death of Christ, and there's no doubt that it does apply. Jesus was the corn of wheat; He was willing to lay down His life; He fell into the ground, was buried, and out of His death and burial and resurrection there came forth much fruit. But some time ago, as I meditated about this, I began to see myself and my fellow believers, each one of us holding in our hand a little corn that God placed there; your gift, your ministry, your talent, something precious because God gave it to you.

You say, "It's mine; I can do it; I know how to cast out demons; I can pray for the sick and they get smitten to the ground, brother. I've got the word of knowledge." It's so nice to hold it in your hand and feel it there and say, "It's mine." But God says, "If you keep it there, that's all you'll have . . . just one little corn." You can put your name on it, you can put your label on it, you can go on claiming it as yours, but you'll never get more.

What's the alternative? Let go! Drop it! "You mean, let my ministry go? Let my talent go? Let my gift go?" Yes, let it go! Let it go right down into the earth and get buried and lost and out of sight. After that you won't own it any longer. But I'll tell you something: God will be responsible for it. And God has guaranteed the fruit.

I believe this is the place to which we're coming. Many of us are going to be faced with this choice. Do I want to propagate myself? Do I want to establish my reputation? Do I want to build my ministry, my outreach, my camp, my youth centre, my deliverance centre? Am I interested in the fact that it's mine? Or if I'm wrongfully challenged and the ownership is disputed, am I willing to say to the wrongful mother, "You take it"? Do I love it or do I love me? A very searching question. Whatever God has given you, I believe there will come a time that He'll ask you to let it go. Drop it. Let it fall.

I know this is registering with some of you! Praise God, you're glad you let it go! I'm glad I've let some things go, too. If I'd gone on carrying them, they would have dragged me down to the ground.

six

Except a Corn of Wheat...

Most preachers are too busy. I'm busy, but I'm not too busy. Did you know that it isn't spiritual to be too busy? It may impress people, but it's not spiritual. God only made you one person, and you'll never do two persons' jobs satisfactorily, no matter how hard you try.

I read a little article by Jamie Buckingham in his church bulletin about his decision to give up doing the "urgent" in order to do the "important." Most preachers are so submerged beneath the urgent, they never get to do the important. One of the most needed prayers in the Bible is in Psalm 90: "Teach us to number our days, that we may apply our hearts unto wisdom." "Teach me how to use my time." That is one of the things that impresses me most about Jesus. He was never flustered. He was never hurried. He was never too busy. Actually, it's an extension of my ego if I make myself indispensable. Most people really don't want to be dispensable. As far as I'm concerned, my greatest triumph is when I can be done without. Then I've succeeded!

I'll tell you a true story which is being out-worked in my life all the time. In June 1971, I went to Seattle, Washington, to take part in a kind of fellowship retreat for ministers. Don Basham was there, Bob Mumford, Charles Simpson, Larry Christenson, Ralph Wilkerson, David DuPlessis, Dennis Bennett, Ern Baxter, and many other nationally known charismatic teachers. It lasted about five days. Every morning and most of the afternoons we were gathered in fellowship, and it was quite an experience. We spent a day and a half talking about demons. We spent two days talking about water baptism. When you've cleared those two hurdles; you've made progress!

But to get so many teachers to the far northwestern corner of the United States was very expensive, and they had no funds from which to draw. So the organisers of the conference said, "Brethren, we promise you nothing, but we'll try to raise the money for your fares." For this purpose they arranged public services every night of the week in five strategically located preaching points in and around Seattle. And they turned loose two or three preachers every night at each point. Well, every one of those places was filled to capacity every night before the meeting ever opened. And the response of the people was tremendous.

When the retreat was over, I stayed on in Seattle to minister in one of the Assembly of God churches just for the weekend. In this way I had the opportunity to hear the local ministers talking together about the meetings. As I had previously pastored a church in Seattle, I knew many of them, and I knew that they were expressing their real opinions. In essence, their comments amounted to this: "In all our memory no meetings have ever made such an impact on the city of Seattle as these meetings." But the comical thing about those meetings from the human standpoint was that they weren't organised to make an impact on the city of Seattle. They were organised to raise the preachers' fares. That's the simple truth!

On Monday morning I found myself in the aeroplane, flying from Seattle to Atlanta, where my next meetings were scheduled. An aeroplane is one of the best places to meditate. The telephone can't reach you, people don't bother you, you just sit back in your seat, alone with your thoughts. As I sat there, I began to say to myself, "Isn't that strange? Meetings that were not planned to make an impact on a city made a greater impact than meetings that were planned for that very purpose." At that moment, the Lord began to speak to me very clearly, not audibly, but quietly and very definitely, and this is what He said: "Now tell me this. With whom did I have more problems – Jonah, or the city of Nineveh?" I thought for a while and then I said, "Lord, when you got Jonah straightened out, you had no problems with Nineveh." And He said "And when I get the preachers straightened out, I'll have no problems with the people!"

Now I can tell that story because I'm a

preacher myself. The Lord didn't say, "When I get the other preachers straightened out...." He said, "When I get the preachers straightened out...." I was included with the rest of them, and I realised that.

After I had reached Atlanta, the Lord continued to deal with me along this line. My meetings there were being held in a hotel. In between two of them I was resting in one of the rooms and my mind was more or less a blank. I find that when our minds are not too active, God can more easily get our attention. As I lay there in that condition, a series of words came to my mind – many of them place names. They were as clear and as vivid as if they had been printed on paper before my eyes. These were the words: "From Cherith to Zarephath; from Zarephath to Carmel; from Carmel to Horeb; and from Horeb into many lives." I knew enough of the Bible to recognise immediately that the words were an outline of the career of Elijah and that the place names represented successive stages in his ministry: from Cherith to Zarephath to Carmel to Horeb.

Then I began to fill in the details in my mind

and saw very plainly that the real climax of Elijah's public ministry was on Mount Carmel. It was there that he gathered all Israel; there he challenged 850 false prophets; there he called down fire from heaven and saw all Israel prostrated on their faces crying, "The Lord, He is the God." If ever any man had a personal, individual triumph, that man was Elijah on Mount Carmel.

But then the Lord showed me that within a few days Elijah was running away from Jezebel, a woman and a witch, and asking God to take away his life. So brief and impermanent was the triumph of Carmel! The next thought that came to me was this: had God answered Elijah's request and taken away his life at that point, Elijah would have died with his task incomplete and without any spiritual successor. There would have been no one to carry on and complete his work. But when he finally got to Horeb and came face to face with God and heard God's plan, it was very different from Elijah's plan.

God said, "Elijah, what are you doing here?" He said, "I've been very jealous for the Lord . . ." and he went on to give a list of all his activities and achievements. The Lord said, in so many words, "I know about that, Elijah, but what are you doing here?" And when Elijah had finished telling the Lord all he'd been doing, the Lord told Elijah what He wanted him to do next. He said, "I want you to anoint three men: Elisha to be prophet in your place. Hazael to be King of Syria, and Jehu to be King of Israel." If you read the subsequent chapters in the Books of Kings, you'll find that those three men who were the product of that interview between God and Elijah on Mount Horeb finished off every task assigned by God to Elijah. Eventually there was nothing left undone. Elijah could not finish the job himself, but he could find his successors and hand it over to them.

As all this passed through my mind, I realised that God was speaking very directly to me. He was showing me that I had two options before me. On the one hand, I could go on doing my own thing, carrying on my own ministry, using the faith and the power that God had given me to whatever extent I was able, and I could achieve some kind of a personal triumph. But I would end without a successor, and there would be no permanent fruit to my ministry. On the other hand, God showed me the alternative: don't be ambitious for yourself, don't promote your own ministry, don't do your own thing – invest in the lives of others. Let them get the credit, let them take over where you have to leave off. Let them be more successful than you are.

I've always been in a certain sense a successful person. I don't say that boastfully, but from way back when I was twelve years old I've been head boy, captain of the school, senior scholar, youngest fellow of the college, all the way through. It's ingrained in my thinking to expect to be successful. But God has shown me there's a higher standard of success. Let that little corn of wheat that you hold in your hand fall to the ground and die. And God will take care of the consequences.

Let me share this with you – I'm possibly the freest person there is because I have let go and let God. I don't care if I never cast out another demon. If God doesn't want me to, I don't mind the least bit. I don't mind if I never conduct another seminar, if I never write another book. If God so leads that I disappear from the public eye, that's all right by me, as long as I've invested what I have where it will do good. I don't even know how much I have; I don't have to know. But what I have I'm willing to give; I'm willing to let it drop. As a result, I'm very, very happy. Truly I'm free. I know what it is to act freely, I know what it is to preach freedom, but the best thing is to be free. And I can say in all sincerity before God, "I'm free!"

7

Letting Go

$\mathcal{S}$ome time ago, I was gripped by the word "secret," as it's used in various places in the Bible.

For instance, in 1 Corinthians 2:7, Paul says, "But we speak the wisdom of God in a mystery…" The RSV renders this, "But we impart a secret and hidden wisdom of God…." So there is a secret wisdom of God; something that's hidden from the minds of most people. For my part, I have a deep desire to acquire that secret, hidden wisdom! Then in Psalm 51:6 David says:

Behold, You desire truth in the inward parts, and in the hidden part You will make me to know wisdom.

Notice the phrase: "wisdom in the hidden part" – or place. Paul was probably referring in 1 Corinthians 2:7 to this wisdom of God that's hidden in a secret place.

To me there is something especially attractive about all this – the secret place, the secret wisdom, the secret knowledge. But there is one condition we have to meet. If a thing is secret, it's hidden – it's out of sight. And so if we want to dwell in that secret place and find that secret wisdom, we ourselves must be willing to be hidden. Our own personality, our own reputation, our own ego will stand in the way. We will have to let them go – to let them fall into the ground and die.

Think about the life of Jesus just for a moment. Since His incarnation as a man, He spent about thirty years in perfect family life, three and a half years in public ministry, and almost 2,000 years in intercession. Are you prepared for that proportion? Do you want real influence? The people that rule the world for God are the intercessors, and most of them are not publicly known at all. Are you willing to bow out?

What was the last public appearance of Jesus

in the eyes of the world? On the cross. Then, when He reappeared in the earth, how did He reappear? In the ministry of His disciples. He dropped into the ground, died, and out came the fruit. Are you willing to do that? Am I willing to do that? Are you holding onto your Isaac? "God, You gave it to me," you say: "It's mine." God says, "Give it back. Put it on the altar. Take the knife." God says, "If you'll give it to Me, in My way, and in My time, when it suits Me, I'll bless it, and multiply it more than your ability to understand or comprehend."

Years ago I told the Lord that I would no longer preach mere religious lectures if I could help it; that when I preached a thing, I'd give the people opportunity to act on the truth I had preached. I feel that I owe it to you to do that. I will not put pressure on anybody, but there must be not a few who are holding on to their Isaacs; who are saying "It's mine, God. I built it up, I established it." Maybe your Isaac is really a literal child that you're holding onto. God says, "Would you let go and let Me?" Or it may be some gift, some ministry or some special situation. If God has really spoken to your heart,

I would encourage you to bring your Isaac and put it on the altar.

Here are some simple words with which to respond:

Dear Lord

You know that I have been unhappy and tense because I have been asserting my own will and claiming to own something which you gave me. That something has been (name that which applies to you; your ministry, a special person, a gift or something else).

I pray that, by your Holy Spirit, you will give me the grace to let go and hand this Isaac over to you. I trust you with the consequences of letting go.

In Jesus' Name AMEN

About the Author

*D*erek Prince (1915–2003) was born in India of British parents. Educated as a scholar of Greek and Latin at Eton College and Cambridge University, England, he held a Fellowship in Ancient and Modern Philosophy at King's College. He also studied several modern languages, including Hebrew and Aramaic, at Cambridge University and the Hebrew University in Jerusalem.

While serving with the British army in World War II, he began to study the Bible and experienced a life-changing encounter with Jesus Christ. Out of this encounter he formed two conclusions: first, that Jesus Christ is alive; second, that the Bible is a true, relevant, up-to- date book. These conclusions altered the whole course of his life, which he then devoted to studying and teaching the Bible.

Derek's main gift of explaining the Bible and its teaching in a clear and simple way has helped build a foundation of faith in millions of lives. His non-denominational, non-sectarian approach has made his teaching equally relevant and helpful to people from all racial and religious backgrounds.

He is the author of over 50 books, 600 audio and 100 video teachings, many of which have been translated and published in more than 100 languages. His daily radio broadcast is translated into Arabic, Chinese (Amoy, Cantonese, Mandarin, Shanghaiese, Swatow), Croatian, German, Malagasy, Mongolian, Russian, Samoan, Spanish and Tongan. The radio program continues to touch lives around the world.

Derek Prince Ministries persists in reaching out to believers in over 140 countries with Derek's teachings, fulfilling the mandate to keep on "until Jesus returns." This is effected through the outreaches of more than 45 Derek Prince offices around the world, including primary work in Australia, Canada, China, France, Germany, the Netherlands, New Zealand, Norway, Russia, South Africa, Switzerland, the United

Kingdom and the United States. For current information about these and other worldwide locations, visit www.derekprince.com.

Books by Derek Prince

Appointment in Jerusalem

At the End of Time

Authority and Power of God's Word

Be Perfect – but How?

Blessing or Curse: You Can Choose

Bought with Blood

by Grace Alone

Called to Conquer

Choice of a Partner, The

Christ's Last Order

Complete Salvation

Declaring God's Word (365 Day Devotional)

Declaring God's Word – 7 Days on Healing

Destiny of Israel and the Church, The

Divine Exchange, The

Doctrine of Baptisms, The

Derek Prince: A Biography (a
Teacher for Our Time)

How to Pass from Curse to Blessing
Husbands and Fathers
If You Want God's Best
Immersion in the Spirit
Judging – When, Why, How
Key to the Middle East, The
Keys to Successful Living
Life-Changing Spiritual Power
Living as Salt and Light
Lucifer Exposed
Marriage Covenant
Orphans, Widows, The Poor and Oppressed
Our Debt to Israel
Pages from My Life's Book
Philosophy, The Bible and the Supernatural
Power in the Name
Power of Communion, The
Power of Faith, The
Power of the Sacrifice, The
Prayers & Proclamations
Praying for the Government
Pride vs. Humility
Promise of Provision, The
Prophetic Guide to the End Times
Protection from Deception

What's so Important About the Cross?
Where Wisdom Begins
Who Is the Holy Spirit?
Why Bad Things Happen to God's People
Why Israel?
Will You Intercede?
You Matter to God
You Shall Receive Power

Derek Prince Ministries Offices Worldwide

DPM – Asia/Pacific

38 Hawdon Street

Sydenham

Christchurch 8023

New Zealand

T: + 64 3 366 4443

E: admin@dpm.co.nz

W: www.dpm.co.nz and www.derekprince.in

DPM – Australia

15 Park Road

Seven Hills

New South Wales 2147

Australia

T: +61 2 9838 7778

E: enquiries@au.derekprince.com

W: www.derekprince.com.au

DPM – Canada
P.O. Box 8354 Halifax
Nova Scotia B3K 5M1
Canada
T: + 1 902 443 9577
E: enquiries.dpm@eastlink.ca
W: www.derekprince.org

DPM – France
B.P. 31, Route d'Oupia
34210 Olonzac
France
T: + 33 468 913872
E: info@derekprince.fr
W: www.derekprince.fr

DPM – Germany
Söldenhofstr. 10
83308 Trostberg
Germany
T: + 49 8621 64146
E: ibl@ibl-dpm.net
W: www.ibl-dpm.net

DPM – Netherlands
Nijverheidsweg 12
7005 BJ Doetinchem
Netherlands
T: +31 251–255044
E: info@derekprince.nl
W: www.derekprince.nl

DPM – Norway
P.O. Box 129
Lodderfjord
N-5881 Bergen
Norway
T: +47 928 39855
E: sverre@derekprince.no
W: www.derekprince.no

Derek Prince Publications Pte. Ltd.
P.O. Box 2046
Robinson Road Post Office
Singapore 904046
T: + 65 6392 1812
E: dpmchina@singnet.com.sg
W: www.dpmchina.org (English)
    www.ygmweb.org (Chinese)

DPM – South Africa
P.O. Box 33367
Glenstantia
0010 Pretoria
South Africa
T: +27 12 348 9537
E: enquiries@derekprince.co.za
W: www.derekprince.co.za

DPM – Switzerland
Alpenblick 8
CH-8934 Knonau
Switzerland
T: + 41 44 768 25 06
E: dpm-ch@ibl-dpm.net
W: www.ibl-dpm.net

DPM – UK
PO Box 393
Hitchin SG5 9EU
United Kingdom
T: + 44 1462 492100
E: enquiries@dpmuk.org
W: www.dpmuk.org

DPM – USA
P.O. Box 19501
Charlotte NC 28219
USA
T: + 1 704 357 3556
E: ContactUs@derekprince.org
W: www.derekprince.org

Lightning Source UK Ltd.
Milton Keynes UK
UKHW020833061219
354840UK00013B/822/P